Shadows of Footsteps
Poetry

Lughano Mwangwegho

Langaa Research & Publishing CIG
Mankon, Bamenda

Publisher:
Langaa RPCIG
Langaa Research & Publishing Common Initiative Group
P.O. Box 902 Mankon
Bamenda
North West Region
Cameroon
Langaagrp@gmail.com
www.langaa-rpcig.net

Distributed in and outside N. America by African Books Collective
orders@africanbookscollective.com
www.africanbookscollective.com

ISBN: 9956-763-32-2

Table of contents

iii

Part I

Reflections

A Prodigal Lover

I yielded to the flattery of your tongue
And eyes which with lies rhyme
When in my ears love songs you sang
And always repeated you loved me in record time
Much as I tried to quench your intemperate lust
As often as your dry throat demanded
You slept out and left me alone to rust
Until you were robbed and left empty handed
Now poor as you are with clothes torn
You tell your story in tears that I should forgive
Sick as you are thin to the bone
You breathe though you still have life to live
Go back to your mistress whom you considered first
To whose house you were a regular guest

The Virgin's Last Moment

Dry leaves whimper
Upon being trodden by casterly winds

Overlooking the twin anthills
Above the chapel's door

Is a big tree
A snake wagging his tongue
Yearning for wine

Which in cups ferment
Comes down the tree
Breaks the door

And along the aisle
Draws his slimy length
Until he coils and dies on the alter

The Harvest Season

Clouds in the sky no longer darken
The harvest season is gone
Dry stalks lying alone in the garden
Whisper when trodden upon
I wait for another while
No smell of rain either
Although dry the soil is fertile
And nothing in it can wither
Until you accept to contend
With any man of your preference
The gossip will not end
We will not be regarded with reverence
As it was done
The day we became one

Love without Borders

Love, true love has no borders
It sees beyond religion, race or tribal roots
And listens only to heavenly orders
That any man with any woman can bear fruits
Love, true love is beyond south or north
As long as a man loves his woman so
And jealously veils her with a wedding cloth
That no other man sees her from head to toe
Love, true love is blind and deaf
It tolerates everything the other does
True love sees beyond beauty and wealth
And accepts whatever the other has
True love
Is shared not in half

Waiting for the Rain

I long for the rains
Not which in drizzles pour

My earth smelt sweet
With the tiny drops
That in drizzles poured

I felt no water drops
Drip into my womb

The new moon is out
Clouds have enveloped it
In their dark arms

This season is for rains
Which in drops pour

Cover me with grass
As I wait for the rains
Which pour not in drizzles

A Letter from Nadzimbiri

I awoke only to catch myself alone
Without the warmth of my groom
Who had disappeared early at dawn
While I slept dead and cold in my room
That he has remarried I have heard
One of those that brothels frequent
Who to the cemetery many a man has led
For death to man is the least lenient
If he waited for a season, he would believe
That with any seed he could still yield
Not everyone on the first night can conceive
Unless another man already tilled her field
And sowed his seed there
While she was asleep and unaware

Walking the Last Mile

A drought stricken rivulet
On whose shores

Grass no longer grows green
Is wide open

Like a fissure on the heel.
Sun burnt cobs

Dangle on the stalks
Once they danced in the wind

When the stalks
Were green and fresh

A Woman's Joy

A woman's joy is short lived
Like sweet sighs painfully heaved
By newlyweds under a dark cloud
When whispers are cold but loud

Her palms are well qualified
Thus to the kitchen confined
To blister but in kind
For he who is always in her mind

He whose heavy hand is a lash
That enjoys her face to smash.
Tears are her only weapon
She wholly relies upon

She was endowed with it
Yet she still concedes defeat

Song of a bride

Those tears dripping from your eyes
As if with the heart you truly weep
Tell your tongue utters nothing but lies
Which anything can hardly reap
I found you in a thick forest
Each to each embracing with a lass
Yet I have never seen you without a dress
As you were, covered only with grass
No one but a foolish bride
Would such a shameful sin forgive
Even for long by her you did abide
Only to mess up on the wedding's eve
No woman with a full life
Would want her well dug with a knife

A dance in the forest

It is in this dense forest
Where night is silent and dark
You leaned over my young breasts to rest
As your chest danced to the beating of my heart
You stole my pride even though I refused
Strange fingers under my camisole
In my womb it rained and you abused
My virginity just to console your lust
I shuddered with fear and in your mouth
My cry suffocated as I heaved your torso in pain
Only to freeze on completing the oath
Letting my tears the pain and the fears drain
To render the well within my womb dry
And prepare me for a maiden birth cry

To My Beloved

Your skin is yielding like a baby's bottom
In such beauty no ailment veils
Draw me near your bosom
It is the heart beat that true love unveils
Let's upon the green grass lie
If only this night my thirst I quench
I will with all the soul love you till I die
And this is all I can pledge
Those women who in the dark gossip
You are to me as a slave wedded
Hardly know all chores are a love's recipe
And a lot is said about a couple that's envied
But do not listen to any body
Or our love will not last a day

In the Garden of Love

From heavens above
Echoed a voice in the garden of love

Eat of all trees in the garden
But the one in the middle it is barren

Drink from all wells all seasons
But the one in the middle for reasons

Whispered a voice in the couple's ears
Who failed to keep a word for years

Barely shielded by the green underbrush
Swooped a thirsty snake from a branch

And drank deep from the middle well
Whence the woman of the tree ate as well

Were it Not for My Wife Bertha

Were it not for my wife Bertha
Whom before I whipped with a wire that dawn
Had refused to give me warm water to bathe
Because she gathers firewood alone
Were it not for Bertha my wife
Who before I chopped her hands that afternoon
Rendering her useless for life
Had refused to cook my favourite mushroom
Were it not for Bertha my ex
Whom before I raped ten times that night
Had sentenced me to forty nights without sex
Denying me the gods given right
I could not have been committed to prison to die
For there's a because for every why

The Night Dance

A fledgling hand it was
That broke the fortified walls
Of a woman's pride

And stroked the tattoos
Deeply engraved on her chest
That in pitch dark night glittered

On nothing but strings of beads
That in her waist sang
She danced for him in the night

And bartered her pride for nothing
For she too drained his strength
And left him empty and weary

Listen to Me

You always come at night when I am asleep
And deafen my ears with your heavy voices
That all my sweet dreams away sweep
And leave behind echoes and noises
Every night you bore me with the same belief
That every man is the head of his family
And no woman can take over even in brief
And the elders look on and nod happily
Now listen to me young man and listen well
You could be the head but I am the heart
To bring you on earth I went through hell
I lost sleep when you were sick and hurt
For without me
You could not be

Desperation

Shall I see thunder again?
Clouds tell it will not rain

When they curl, darken and gather
They uncurl, lighten and scatter

With sweat I will water the flower
Every minute and every hour

That I must pride myself on
When on the stem she blossoms

A Teen Mother

A hot season again
The moon shone bright.
Fear-smitten, pain pricked

Through the bone marrow
As he pierced his tongue
To the depths of my flesh

Shards of virginity
Like dry leaves on the ground
Sing the cord-breaking songs

Sweet Is Your Voice

Sweet is your voice
Drifting in the ripples of air
Blown without a single noise
Yet able to draw a distant stare
Your figure, an art of a born sculptor
Whose crafty hands are likened to no tool
Kindle a desire in many a hopeless suitor
Wishing to own you like a kingly stool
I will not let my eyes succumb to sleep
However long may be the night
For you don't quench thirst with a sip
When a full calabash is in sight
With beer brewed to perfection
Beyond every man's expectation

Weep Not, Flower

In the middle of the forest
A flower did grow
A lean figure she was
The true image of she that bore

Thirsty bees
Perching as if under order
Stroke the knobs
On her stem growing fonder

Deep into the stalk
With their stings they did imbibe
Breaking the bead strings
That on her bestowed pride

As the only flower
Whose nectar was never stolen-
Sucked dry she withered
And wept over her virginity broken

The Well So Deep

A female bedfellow trumpets loud
Though breathing in a loudhailer

She can hardly hear
Ripples of the stream
That through the twin hills
Snake down to a forest below

Draining off loads of dirt
That along its way
Await the next rains

Are There Seeds in the Granary?

Are there seeds in the granary
With this expanse of land to tally?

The land scarcely soaks in the rain
And wears green like a mountain

The clouds scudding apart
To the land rain cannot grant

Until scorching rays disappear
And to thunder's orders adhere

Part II

African experiences

The African Girl

Grandma says I must get used to fire
Because my hands were made to cook all my life
I go to the kitchen and laugh at her satire
Because a man too can cook for his wife
Grandma says I must not sleep with underwear on
Because my womb was made only to bear children
I go to the bedroom and cry on my own
Because I too can show I have the brain
Grandma says I must fetch wood from the forest
Because my head is for carrying fire-wood
I go to the bush to avoid hearing the rest
For I am a stranger in her neighbourhood
And my ideas are too foreign
Without anything she can learn

Unanswered Questions

Who takes the farmer's harvest
When he has nothing to eat?
The sun burns the cobbler's feet
Who wears his shoes?

Who sleeps in the builder's house
When he sleeps on open air?
The tailor's belly is bare
Who wears his clothes?

Who eats the meat the butcher sells
When he eats leaves of ground-nuts?
The carpenter sits on reed-mats
Who sits on his stools?

Who enjoys rights of a freedom fighter
When he dies?
A dying soldier in agony cries
Whose freedom does he fight for?

A Woman's Weapon

The first breath I drew was not of joy
My suffering had just begun
I have been reduced to a soft toy
And I have become a slave of man
He whips me with his long hand
Until I am bruised and pale
He tills in another land
When in my womb his seeds fail
My voice is in my heart hidden
I hush my temper and suffer in silence
For I was told my office is the kitchen
Scalds and burns are my licence
My tears are my only weapon
I wholly rely upon

Old Woman, Come Near

Old woman, come near
And listen to what I say:

Do you also believe
Where there's a path, there's a way

However narrow
It widens by the end of the day?

This girl is only ten
But has led many men astray

Some, her father's age
Have left their wives and fallen prey

And in spite of themselves
They force themselves in any way

In Two Verses

He who takes a woman for a wife
Brings misery to his heart

But she who takes a man for life
Brings joy to her hut

The Drought

There's no millet with which to appease
The gods we have forsaken for years
There's nothing to offer the river spirits
Who quench thirst with their tears
We rely on the after-harvest we glean
From heaps of dry barren stalks
And the river once fresh and clean
That snakes at the bottom most
Our hearts have been rendered poor
When we sniff around we smell death
When we beat the empty drum tears pour
And sink to the depth of earth
To announce another drought
If our offerings are still of doubt

Growing With Time

At dawn when cockerels crow with gaiety
A baby is born
To fulfill a woman's noble duty

At midday when the sun is high in the sky
A child in his salad days
Enjoys life to fullness though he will never die

At dusk when the sun disappears behind a crest
An old man bent on a walking stick
Walks slowly toward the grave to rest

Of old Age and Sorcery

She stands there
Gnawing at nothing but toothless gums
Her cold feet cracked and bare
And in her belly hunger roaring like drums

Casting a long stare
At her field of yams
She has left under nobody's care
She coughs into her palms
And rubs the spit in her unkempt hair

Like a child in her mother's arms
She has nothing of her own to declare
But rivers of tears to fill empty dams
And pain she can hardly bear

In Spite of Oneself

In the mortuary is a doctor
Deceased after conceding defeat to some disease

In the dock is a judge
In court with cases of different sorts

In custody is a police officer
Guilty of burglary while on duty

Letter from Exile

Is the river still flowing
Or with the summer heat it dried?
The fig along the path, is it bearing
Or hot winds scorched its womb and it died?

And my child, a full-grown woman
And no longer bathing in the rain?
Is my wife without a man
And waiting for my return?

Mary's Black Cloth

She moaned her only child
Grief dripped from her womb

The pangs that on the night of lullaby
Rendered her eyes sleepless
Pinched her lungs
With sharp pliers

The only child who suckled her breasts
Laden with pride

Had his ribs shattered
Flesh thronged with alligator skin
And body hung on the shaft

The Rite of Passage

I hear drums rumble
Loud they echo and re-echo in unison
In the hut elderly women mumble
Unaware though that I have arisen
I hear every low voiced word they utter
Within the drum-beats that my heart smite
And like a synthetic thunder thunder
Cracking the earth with its might
My ears should deafen with piercing cries
Of little girls outgrowing youth
Who are not women until a man's sighs
Echo in their wombs and nipples on their chest jut
And when everything is over
With a cloth their thighs they cover

Whenever I Try

Whenever I try I fail
Like the seeds that on the rock fell
And forth brought nothing to being
That there's no longer anything to veil

I now fail to try
Since the seeds on the rock still lie
And there's nothing they can forth bring
So I just sleep and cry

Confessions

We have eyes but cannot see beyond the nose
And we think slowly though we have no brain
Our weapon is tears and when we lose
We are voluble like a frightened hen

We are listeners and you speakers
Who throw everything we say in a dustbin
We are learners and you teachers
Who teach us everything while we lie supine

We are cooks and you eaters
Who would dump us if food was underdone
We are diggers and you reapers
Who only appear when growing season is gone

Mikuyu Prison

A door opens, November first, past three o'clock
Within the four walls I scatter my eyes
A stench of wine, sweat and cigarette smoke
Drifting in whirlwinds of praise songs arise
Men wearing out with unquenchable lust
Brandishing hard tails, others lying on the floor
Heavily infested with thirsty lice and dust
Embrace me with a welcome never felt before
My tongue grows numb as I try to barter
Stories from outside for food but in earnest
For some it was theft, yet others rape or murder
And had fled but were caught the earliest
As for me, the court found me guilty
Of winking at a woman constable on duty

Of Wisdom & Lies

This man thinks to have grey hair
Is a sign of wisdom
But it is just a scare
That the grey-haired do not lie

This man thinks to have a bald head
Is a sign of wisdom
But it is just how he was made
That he must not walk under a bare sky

This man thinks to have no teeth
Is a sign of wisdom
But it is just a myth
That will take many years to die

This man thinks to have wrinkles on the face
Is a sign of wisdom
But it is just a disgrace
That it has taken him long to say bye

Dying Young

Along Hannover street
I smelt love
From their empty hearts

I was stunned
By beads which around their waists

Holily sang-
Weaned yellow leaves

Embrace the soil
And rot in haste

Trial of a Prostitute

Your flesh but bones
Will rot and turn into dust.

Said the judge

Kill me not with stones
Such death is unjust

Answered she with a grudge

But not to those that kill
And plead guilty.

Said he furiously

He failed to pay his bill-
He should not have done it truly…

Give me a glass of beer
That I may forget all that is gone.

Answered she curiously

Stricken with fear
She spoke in undertone

Mama, Sing me the Song

For my late mother, Ellen

If I beat the drum
Will you sing the song, mama?
If I strike the hide of ram
Will I make your frail heart shudder?
Although your lungs are no longer strong
And your voice too weak to sing
You can sing me the song
Which tell of your early beginning
Although your charm disappears in furrows
Folding down by the years
You can sing the song, so mellow
Even to the deafest ears
You can regain the youthful strength
And sing the song at length

The African Child

He was dug out of the ant-hill
Where the cord is cut like cane
And buried at the mother's will.
The child's first cry was of pain

Incise tattoos of reverence
On the hunter's leg
Tattoos of perseverance
On the wood-fetcher's neck

Turn of Events

I danced for men in local the bar
Just to pay for your fees
I drew water for madams from afar
Just to fend for your needs
I sold my livestock at a low cost
That you may not die of hunger or thirst
I worked in fields even during frost
That you may not sleep in a nest
You have been taken to the alter
That he alone enjoys the shepherd's pie
You have married somebody's daughter
That she alone inherits everything when you die
As I still languish in poverty
Without food or property

Children of War

They hail the morning dew
With dry tongues
And running noses stricken with flu
And nobody seems to care

They roam around the neighbourhood
In small gangs
Upsetting dust bins for food
As women pitifully stare

Although touched by their plight
And feeling pinches of birth pangs
They cannot host them even for a night
For reasons they cannot share

Jezebel

She was endowed with unequalled beauty
Whose smile was never in quarter
And her crafty hands always committed to duty
She was a woman worth taking to the alter
Contented with creation, she never craved for more
But was no match to any woman young or old
Second only to she her granny bore
Until by heavens early she was called
As grieved men wear sombre faces
Joyous women ululate at the demise
Of a woman inflicted with jezebel's curse
A woman who under disguise
Made friends with any woman far or near
Only to sleep with their men without fear

Her Silver Lining

You pour scorn on her looks
And call her names no pen can write
You nauseate at the smell of what she cooks
Even when seasoned you still refuse a bite
You laugh at her bow legs
And how she drags her feet when walking
You call her eyes two ostrich eggs
That only look but see nothing
Why do you keep her in your house
And still call her your only wife?
Is it the warmth underneath her blouse
That you want near you all your life?
Or the cold spring under her dress
That often quenches your thirst with grace?

Around Chikangawa Forest

Sucked dry, withered nipples
Wean away leaves

Scattered on the ground
In cold embrace
They dry in the glow
Where woods burn

Charcoal burners
Hard pound the bones
Fresh like a new bloom

Their smothered mouths
Discharge ashes

The Twig

When a tree is felled down by thunder
The leaves dry and the stem rots
But cannot be buried under
For when it rains a fresh twig shoots
It grows and dons in the same leaves
As those of the mother tree dead
Yet to her norms it refuses to cleave
For with them farewell she bade
What tomorrow holds for the twig so fresh
Is known only by he that the seedling
Once kept and later buried in the earth
And with all the care let it grow
Without a single wound from his hoe

Daughter, Unlike Her Mother

You are the true image of my wife
And her beauty like a mirror reflects on your face

I hear last gasps of her breath drumming in your heart
Her laughter drowning in a pool of your tears
And cries of birth pangs echoing in the hut
As she bade farewell on the night she gave you life

Although we buried her and celebrated the life
She granted you out of grace

I cry when you fail to fit in her hat
And hate how you have lived over the years
For I thought as a kitten is as a cat
You would be as my beloved wife

Blessed is the Widow

Though married I sleep like a maiden
With cloths on and a pillow held in my arms
Stories from the market-place fly over the roof
And leave behind choking smoke in the neighbourhood

His sharp hoe can plough the whole Garden of Eden
And where it lands it leaves holes like dams
To the grief of she who only wanted proof
For she just spoiled her womanhood

What shall man gain
When he takes all the women to the bluegums
And get honey from their beehives without a glove
Just to prove his manhood?

Blessed is the widow who despite praying in vain
To have someone who can be oiling her palms
Knows her husband sleeps in the grove
And he cares less about her livelihood

Part III

Voices from within

African Pride

For my father, Nolence Moses

You are well versed with many a foreign word
And you can converse even better than the owners
You crossed many graves to see the world
And returned donning a cloth of honors

Your name is well known far and wide
For telling the white man off in his very eyes
To free your village where we sing with pride
For we too had had enough of his ideas

Tell every child there's no pride in being called Moses
And stammering in one's mother tongue
Tell them there's no pride in embracing foreign mores
While they are still black and young

The Second Coming

It was not in Virgin Mary's womb
Where the child was conceived
It was not in a man's tomb
Where he was buried as it is believed

Being a true son of earth
On whom the gods bestowed prowess
To cast doubts out of those without faith
He was endowed with rain-making powers

The cross where he was hanged and cursed
Spoke of his second coming
Dark clouds wove in haste
And raced westerly without returning

Through the Grapevine

I have heard through the grapevine
That on the roof tops of huts and flats
A man who trekked to the East and returned in vain
Is flying high newfangled flags
Through the grapevine I have heard it all
A man well taught in foreign schools
Is leaving the kingly stool to his sibling of four
Whose all children also await the same stool
Although I have heard it through the grapevine
I have not heard it in half
Neither have I heard it while sipping wine
I have heard it and am waiting for a last laugh:
He who will laugh the loudest
Will raise the flag the highest

A Song for Martyrs

How long shall we sing in agony
About they who this land fought for
And the voiceless many
Hardly known near or far?
About them we sing in good faith:
Thunderous beats and loud choruses
Echo in the wombs of earth
And ripples of tears perform dances
We praise their bravery and pain
That chains of slavery undid
And dethroned the settlers' reign
Riddled with torture and greed
We sing about they who bled
They who fought to their end

The Aftermath

From a distance some settler
Sank his teeth into a turkey's flesh
As we awaited the bone that fell later
Than our hunger imagined

We scrambled and picked a fight
And bathed each other in warm blood
We fought endless battles throughout the night
And the bone lay still on the ground

And now whistles of men milking cows
No longer drift in the morning winds
Only shadows of the aged pushing ploughs
In maize fields remain of the village

Chit-chatting from women gathering firewood
No longer echo in the forest
Only widows wandering in the neighbourhood
Tell what a skeleton the warfare left

In the Shadows of Slavery

I was on the coast basking with my children
When a fleet of ships with merchants aboard docked
In their bags were spices and millet grain
Which for slaves they bartered without bargain

I saw the ships with my children disappear
Their faces with despair and anger cloaked
Yet their songs of protest so loud and clear
As they headed to the unknown sphere

Aboard tanks they shared my land among themselves
And scrambled for oil, diamond and gold
In whose mine fields my children worked as slaves
Who owned no house but slept in caves

For many years they offered their labor
Till every gem and oil to the foreign land they sold
And behind left neighbor fight against neighbour
For border marks drawn along the other's harbor

Just as everyone thought they had gone forever
Aboard chartered planes they came again
And uttered speeches that got our favor
And brainwashed even those that seemed clever

Told not to do anything without their consent
Or their economy would go down the drain
My children appraised their arrival as godsend
Only to realize their money had been equaled to a cent

It is....

It is unholy
To offer a sacrifice of millet to spirits
But godly
To give tithe to priests at the church

It is illiteracy
To speak in mother tongues
But supremacy
To speak in English, Portuguese or French

It is uncivilized
To tell folktales of our forefathers
But modernization
To recite poetry by dead famous poets

It is nonsense
To heal a disease with a concoction of roots
But science
To heal the same with tablets or syrup

It is mythology
To fly in reed-woven baskets
But technology
To fly in space-crafts or parachutes

The Grass is Weeping

That the grass is weeping is known only by a few
Whose hearts with fear are gripped
The grass is soaked to the root with fresh dew
Which like winter drizzles dripped
But its voice is muffled by elephant hooves
That hard the wet ground pound
And whose noisy tramps echoing in the groves
Fell weak trees to the ground
What men of great wisdom prophesy
Is full of many a saying
One of which is once beaten twice shy
Which to he whose brain is decaying
Is just a phrase
He can easily erase

Hell Him

Hell the king, hell the father, hell him

From village girls bathing in the river
To learned women in offices
From young boys watering crops not to wither
To men in the hills offering sacrifices

Hell him

Hell the king, hell the father, hell him

From beggars roaming about in the streets
To pastors preaching the word in the church
From vendors moving about selling sweets
To officers at road blocks conducting a search

Hell him

The Last Laugh

When you took our land
And left us buried in pain and tears
The land we later tilled with bare hands
And gnawed at our teeth in fear
When we worked in your cane fields
And watered every ridge with tears and sweat
Only to get nothing from the yields
Everyone felt all was well and sweet
It is now time to unleash venom of anger
And take back what belongs to us
We have for long died of hunger
When in our land you grew grass
We shall take every millimetre of our land
Whether it is fertile or full of sand

When it Pours

When it pours
Men have a

Bargain. Women die in
Pain. After the
Rain, tears

Graze the soil. In a
Maze the children cry and

Gaze as
Days pass

The Rain

The earth is dancing
To thunder roaring in the horizon
And like disco lights lightening
Is flashing with reason

Clouds in the sky
Are dark and pregnant
Birds are heading back to their nests
As a downpour is eminent

A woman, bag of millet
Strapped on her back, bare and dirty
Disappears into the bush
Leaving behind a crawling baby

The crippled, waiting for a turn look on
As boys armed with spears
Drink from dry wells of old women
Under orders from local beers

Young girls are goods carriers
Or sex slaves
Their fathers are dead
And buried in unmarked graves

When the rain is over
Rivers of blood flow everywhere
And vultures come out to feed on corpses
Scattered here and there

Shadows of Footsteps

She was bred by a black woman
Who never leaves a child hungry or lonely
And feeds him breast milk only
Until dry her breasts run

She has incisions on her forehead
And on her two big toes
They are not ordinary cuts but tattoos
A symbol of true womanhood

Strings of seed beads rattle on her waist
And around her neck
She cannot let the strings break
Lest she render her dignity waste

She is the envy of town girls
Who scramble for bras in clothes stores
Her breasts are not held by camisoles
Yet they stand upright like twin hills

She is a replica of an angel
Whose radiant face never glows with oil
And dark skin fashioned with clay soil
Is never softened with any pricey gel

Each day she gets up before dawn
That she may finish her chores in time
And while dawn is still in its prime
She is in the garden hoeing, all alone

When she and her man are back from the fields
She confines herself to the kitchen
While he rests beside a cage of chickens
Pondering over how he can sell the yields

She draws water from a distant river
At times from a well far apart
Yet she still carries the bucket with art
And gets home without dropping a litre

When she is not dancing traditional dances
Or pounding grains
She is gathering fire-wood with friends
Often walking long distances

When her husband calls she kneels
And never looks him in the face
Not out of fear but in grace
As it is only he who her sexual desires heals

She apologises to her better half
To avoid a feud that may just take long
Even if it was he that was in the wrong
And that's how they mend the gulf

She only reads the letters a b and f
And hardly counts the numbers one to six
Despite all that she can still barter her millet seeds
With a piece of cloth or a calf

Colonizing the mind: modernity & civilization

She despises mats made of reeds
And sleeps on cushions
She dons in western fashions
And hates clothing made of hides

She covers her feet with shoes
And laughs at my bare feet
She sternly refuses rat meat
And prefers cross-bred fruits

She denounces roots of the bush
And takes aspirin when she is ill
When speaking to elders she refuses to kneel
Always saying she is in a rush

She prefers tall buildings of Bombay
Whose walls glitter like glass
To one stair huts thatched with grass
Whose walls wear dark and red clay

She enjoys the history of settlers
And ignores the history of black heroes
Who spent years in prisons
Or passed on in the hands of their jailors

She shuns the company of other girls
And likes watching western films
Or listening to church hymns
And render a deaf ear to folktales

She has toasted bread for breakfast
With a cup of juice, guava or orange
She refuses to eat porridge
She says it is for pet cats

She has a taste for fashion;
She hates her brown skin
She wants to look like a white queen
Who burns the skin with pricey lotions

She dyes her hair brown
She hates it short and dark...
She is always drugged and drunk
And sleeps around with men in town

She refuses to use a latrine
And relieves herself in a white w/c
Where she is able to see
Whether there was blood in her urine

She wets her lips with John's tongue
And brands my norms moth-eaten...
She applauds chemical fertilizers from Britain
And disparages cow dung

Her husband is in police custody
He slept with her without consent
He pleads she is his wife and he is innocent
But the officers have opened a rape case as told

She has taken her husband to court
To have their marriage nullified
She says she is no longer satisfied

Yet all she wants is to get everything the man bought

She snubs me for having many children
And tells me to take a contraceptive
She calls extended families primitive
And no longer calls me her brethren

She scorns whenever we meet in the streets
And openly calls me a witch
She worships at a Presbyterian church
And refuses to deify the ancestral spirits

She dresses like a Hollywood star
Tight shorts and a long jacket...
And when she is going to the market
She goes by a car

She has dragon tattoos on her chest
And she laughs at the incisions on my forehead
Engraved with a razor blade
And the bead strings rattling around my waist

Printed in the United States
By Bookmasters